TRAVELERS FROM THE OLD COUNTRY: MAKING IT IN AMERICA

Half Page Title

Travelers from the Old Country:
Making It in America
Emma Reichwald Schultz

Title Page

Emma Reichwald Schultz

C/O 3900 N Estabrook Parkway #141

Shorewood, WI 53211

414-699-3612

DuaneESchultz@gmail.com

Travelers from the Old Country:
Making It in America

Approximately 13,000 words

:

TRAVELERS FROM THE OLD COUNTRY: MAKING IT IN AMERICA

EMMA REICHWALD SCHULTZ

Glassystone Books

Copyright Page

**Travelers from the Old Country:
Making It in America**

Copyright © 2023 Emma Reichwald Schultz

All rights reserved. No part of this book may be reproduced or used in any manner without the prior written permission of the copyright owner, except for the use of brief quotations in a book review.

To request permissions, contact DuaneESchultz@gmail.com.

Hardcover: ISBN 979-8-9874571-4-6
Paperback: ISBN 979-8-9874571-5-3
EBook: ISBN 979-8-9874571-6-0
Library of Congress Number: 2023905338

Edited by Duane Schultz; Darya and Tina, EBook Launch Editors

Cover, Full moon rising over a green meadow, by Ann Lowe

Book layout by Duane Schultz

Cover Design and Dust Jacket by the Miblart Team

All photos are public domain or from the author's archive collection

DuaneESchultz@gmail.com
DuaneESchultz.org

Dedication

As I am fortunate to have five grandchildren and seven great-grandchildren; this work is dedicated to them

so they can look back and read about the olden times as seen through my eyes and experiences.

I also dedicate this book to my grandparents, parents, sisters, brothers and their families.. They were so

helpful in getting me to adulthood with a positive influence and making me a healthy and upbeat person

throughout my life.

Table of Contents

List of Graphics..page 5

Preface..page 9

Introduction..page 10

Chapter 1—My Mother's Journey to America............................page 11

Chapter 2—My Father's Journey to America.............................page 19

Chapter 3—Gustav and Paulina..page 27

Chapter 4—Herman's Story..page 37

Chapter 5—Farming Times...page 40

Chapter 6— Stories from my Family with Adolph......................page 57

Chapter 7—Reflections: An Open Letter to My Family...............page 62

About this Book..page 65

About the Author..page 66

List of Graphics

Full moon rising over a green meadow, public domain released by Ann Lowe-cover

Picture of the ship the Fredrick de Grosse Public Domain------------------------page13

Picture children playing in steerage, public domain-------------------------------page 14

Paulina's confirmation picture, with her father, mother, and brothers----------page 16

Picture of Gottlieb Desterhoft--page 18

Loading logs from the Oconto County Historical Society------------------------page 22

Blackwell Logging Camp; Gustav in his half apron, as assistant cookie--------page 24

Gustav in center of the picture, skidding logs with the team--------------------page 26

Loading logs from the NY Public Library--page28

Gustav and Paulina's wedding picture----------page 31

Silhouette of farm animals, public domain----------page 32

Hildegarde and Gustav harvesting beets with the horse team----------page 35

Old time bottles & home remedies, New York Public Library----------page 36

Gustav farming with his team of horses----------page 40

Bean field, public domain picture----------page 41

Emma and Norman, picking beans and fighting off the bees----------page 42

Picture of grain field & grain shock, public domain----------page 46

Grandma Ida standing in her yard----------page 48

Picture of horse and sleigh, public domain----------page 53

Emma and Adolph; Dean and Duane----------page 58

Preface and Introduction

When I started this story, it was originally just the story of my parents, their journey to America from Prussia, and the start of their lives in northeastern Wisconsin. I then added memories from when I was a kid growing up. My life, like that of many others, included trials and tribulations of the times as well as the joys and pleasures of family and friends. I shared these stories with my extended family at our family reunion in 2015. Upon the urging of my sons, Duane and Dean, I have now come up with this final version

I felt it was important to add the story of Herman, a friend of the family, and this is recounted in Chapter 4. His story has its own sense of tragedy and is part of that giant patchwork quilt of how people tried their best to make it in America. It features the layering of joy, pain, love and tragedy all of which so often intersect while slicing and dicing the human condition.

The Travelers from the Old Country: Making It in America

Just before the turn of the twentieth century, across the former German state of Prussia and other areas of Eastern Europe, the dreaded pogroms (mob attacks directed at Jews) started up again. In the area of Warsaw, poverty, unrest, and rising anti-Semitic violence sent people on the move. The pogroms were a scourge, with rampant attacks carried out steadily from the early 1800s.

These attacks were not simply a product of that time, as they were documented as early as the 1200s. It has always been easy to blame societal problems on minority groups, especially if they have no power, wealth, or influence. Jewish people encountered and endured these attacks, as did the Romani people, and indeed early Christians felt them as well. African Americans have experienced violence against them for hundreds of years right here in the United States, as well as other minorities coming to America: the Irish, Chinese, Japanese (in fact, other Asians as well) and Spanish speakers. Indeed, it seems as if anyone with a different language, religion, skin tone, or belief system has been a target for abuse and violence at some point in history. It can clearly be seen by the abhorrent treatment given to Indigenous peoples from the first contact with Europeans down to the present time.

It's within this context that we follow the travels of Pauline and her family, and Gustav with his brother, to America. They begin life anew, followed by Gustav and Pauline meeting, marrying, and making a family.

I

My Mother's Journey to America

Gottlieb Desterhoft and Ida Levine were well aware of the ongoing attacks on Jewish communities even as children. In 1890, Gottlieb had married a beautiful Jewish girl, Ida Levine, and they lived in or near what is now Pabianice, Poland, just west of Warsaw. At that time, the country of Poland had ceased to exist, as it had been partitioned by the region's superpowers and was known as Prussia. By late 1901, Gottlieb and Ida heard once again the rumblings of bullying toward the Jewish community in general and perhaps aimed at them directly as well.

The year was 1903, and Gottlieb and Ida Desterhoft had a family with two children; Ferdinand was eleven years old, and Paulina, born in April 29, 1894, was nine. Despite Ida being pregnant with their third child, they made a plan to leave and go to America. The threats were grave enough that they planned to just pick up and flee.

This was a challenge as they had no money and it meant separating from all their friends, neighbors, and relatives. It would have been a tearful goodbye to all, with little likelihood of ever seeing one another again. The dream of opportunity and freedom in the new country was the driving force to make this journey a reality.

There were mixed feelings stirring in their hearts. The knowledge that they would never be able to return was scary, and unknown fears and challenges certainly lay ahead. They soon broke the news to Ida's closest sister, Mathilda Zeltkie. When Mathilda heard about this move, she made Ida promise to write and stay in contact. (This was only a figure of speech since Ida could not write one word.) She also said she would get word to their other sister, Louise, who had married a man by the name of Alex Zinn. They had two sons, Albert and Alex Jr., and there was no chance that they could ever leave, as Louise's husband was now serving in the Czar's Russian Army. Gottlieb had already served his military service obligation to the czar.

Finally, in the early spring of 1903, with one trunk full of clothes and bedding and a few packs each would carry, they started for the German border. Their plan was to get to the port in Bremen and then board a ship for America. It turned out that their timing was fortunate because later that year the pogroms again broke out in mass across the region with an increasing tide of violence toward Jewish communities. Gottlieb certainly loved Ida and his children to undertake such a perilous journey. His strong feelings for Ida and their family made this a great love story.

It is not known if they followed the river, the rail, or the road routes to the West, and we don't know where or how they crossed the border. It is assumed that most travel was done by night because a pass was needed to even go from one town to another. Unless you paid someone to write up a false passport, there was no way to leave. The money required for fake passes likely cut into the precious little money they had to begin with. As always, it was a struggle to provide food for the children, and Ida needed to keep up her strength. Sometimes they were given rides by wagons hauling hay or joined others who were traveling on the roads. The days and nights extended to several months in their journey to Bremen, their port of departure. Through their persistence and strong will, they finally reached Bremen and their ship, *The Fredrich de Grosse*.

It should be noted that the ship itself has an amazing story to tell. Originally launched in 1896, it was known for its transatlantic trips to America. In 1900, the Kaiser sent the ship to China to assist in putting down the Boxer Rebellion. When World War I broke out, it was seized and brought to America, repaired, and renamed the *USS Huron*. It had a major role as a troop transport ship carrying 21,000 soldiers to France during the war and then returning 22,000 troops back to America after hostilities ended.It was amazing that even with those three major roles given the ship that in 1903 the Desterhoft family boarded it for their travel to America.

Although we don't know for sure, it is a good guess that while crossing the Atlantic, Paulina and her family were passengers in steerage, given their limited resources. This meant that they did not have premium accommodations or even a cabin for the trip over to America. Perhaps, as shown here, Paulina was among the children who invented games to pass the time. After encountering deplorable conditions during their month-long passage over the Atlantic Ocean, they finally arrived at Ellis Island on July 12, 1903. Ida was nine months pregnant, and while they were quarantined, she gave birth to their second son. They named him Emil.

Somewhere along the way, somebody had given them the name of some small settlement in Northeastern Wisconsin where people spoke their language. It seemed to Gottlieb that they called the

TRAVELERS FROM THE OLD COUNTRY: MAKING IT IN AMERICA

place Underhill. Perhaps it was Mosling or Gillett. Anyway, they decided to travel there. What did they have to lose?

It was late July before they left the East Coast, and it was difficult for them to later remember how they existed or even what they ate. After a thorny journey, they arrived in Oconto by ship and then traveled west by train to the town of Gillett.

After arriving in Gillett, they found work at the Great Northern Pail Factory in town. They were able to save a small amount of money and purchase eighty acres of land, just south of Gillett. The land was entirely wooded and not too far from a river with two creeks running through the property. When they moved to the land it was wilderness, just trees and forest with underbrush. At first, they camped out and cut trees, building a shack and a small barn.

They walked to Green Bay for supplies. Because there was no road and only a blazed trail, they were kept on track by watching for the axe marks on the trees. It was a two-day trip, and they slept over at a halfway house along the way. The supplies that they brought home were whatever they could carry, as they didn't have a pack animal or horse to help with the load. The cabin they built in the first year was now their home, and it was a place where they could begin to live without the fear that had clutched their hearts in Europe.

Unfortunately, about a year later, a fire burned everything in the home. This was definitely a setback for them and their dreams. The children could not attend school because they were needed to help cut the trees to build their next log house. After much hard work, they did rebuild and made a cozy home. Then Gottlieb found work on the railroad being built from Green Bay to southern Wisconsin. Ida was also pregnant again. This baby brother was born in Gillett, in 1906, and they named him Gust. They had also purchased chickens to start their farm. The hens laid eggs both to hatch and for the family to eat, and they also added a cow for milk and butter.

Life at last was good. They had joined the St. John's Lutheran Church in Gillett when they arrived in the area, and this became their home for worship and celebrating joyous events, such as baptisms of newborn babes, marriages, and confirmations, while sharing the grief of death at the funerals of their beloveds. A great event in Paulina's life was her own confirmation as seen here with her father and her mother at her side, her older brother, Ferdinand, and her little brothers, Emil and Gust standing in front.

TRAVELERS FROM THE OLD COUNTRY: MAKING IT IN AMERICA

Ida became pregnant again, and life seemed to get easier after the next baby, a boy named Albert, was born. Food was a bit more plentiful, and Gottlieb and Ida were able to clothe and feed the family more easily. They had planted a garden and gradually grew their flock of chickens and started a herd of cows.

Paulina had turned nineteen during the spring of 1913. She was never able to attend school because of the need for her assistance to care for her siblings and help with the workload around the homestead. She never did learn to completely read. However, she taught herself enough to get by and could sign her name as well. All her life when she was cooking she had to memorize all the recipes. She was also clear on the priority and importance of schooling. She told everyone, "Stay in school, do your homework, and keep your reading and math skills up to the grade."

The year of 1913 was expecting to be a prosperous one, but suddenly Gottlieb became ill. Where would the money for a doctor come from if Gottlieb could not work? His sickness was no small thing, and after months of illness, he died on August 28, 1914. This left Ida with some real problems. How could she clear land needed to add to the farm? When they came to this Gillett–Pulcifer area, it was all wooded. So much work was left unfinished. Who would do it all?

2

My Father's Journey to America

In the 1880s, somewhere in the eastern part of Poland (that time known as Prussia), in the Town of Niechalsdorut (Nichelsdorf, now Nikielkowo) near Olsztyn, the family of Carl and Bertha (Buyak) Reichwald were farmers eking out an existence with a large family and a limited-sized land plot. The land was sandy and the soil was poor for growing crops. Most people lived in barn houses, as was typical of their German ancestry. The farm buildings were clustered together alongside their neighbors, making a village. The Reichwald family was no different, as the acreage of their farm was small. Sixteen acres was the allotted size of each farm in that area with the actual farmland located on the outskirts of the village proper. The cows were taken to the rich man's woods each morning after milking and watched by the young men of the family, including Gustav. The cows grazed over the day and then were brought home for milking in the late afternoon. The family grew over the years to include seven children: Adolph, Emil, Paulina, August, Gustav, Nathalie and Robert. The close quarters of the home brought a need to find some employment and living options for the children as they grew to adulthood. What could be done?

August, who was born in 1890, was now growing to be a high-spirited young man with a quick temper. He and Gustav, who was three years younger, were close and always sided together against anyone who wanted an argument or to get into a fist fight. At age seventeen, August was sent to be an apprentice to the village blacksmith. Their brother Emil left for the United States of America. Their sister Pauline's husband, Julius Lehman, also went along on the journey.

This left Adolph and Gustav to do the farm work. Robert was too young to be included on the work crew. Over the next three years, Adolph showed his authority in every way possible and lorded it over his brothers. This brought much disharmony to the family. When Gustav reached his seventeenth birthday on February 3, 1910, he went into the village to talk to August. He told him he was going to America. What was there to look forward to here? There was the required military service to the czar and then what would be next? Coming back home would mean a life of what? The farm surely could not support three families if he, August, and Adolph were all to marry. August was shocked. Where would Gustav get enough money to travel? How would he get a pass to leave? Yes, he could obtain one for a visit, but to stay? August decided if Gustav was going, he would go too! Surely, they could figure it out. Gustav cautioned him with, "Let's keep it quiet for a while, August, until we complete the full plan with all the angles worked out."

TRAVELERS FROM THE OLD COUNTRY: MAKING IT IN AMERICA

A month went by, and the brothers' unrest continued to show. Emil and brother-in-law Julius returned from America discouraged, but that did not dampen Gustav's and August's spirits. They became ever more determined by the week. When Gustav approached his father with the idea, he was met with very stern disapproval. "And where will you get the money? That is what I'd like to know!"

Several more weeks passed and again, the subject surfaced. Gustav, in a heated discussion with his dad threatened to go to his uncle and ask for help. His dad asked for a bit more time to think this over A few weeks later, his dad offered to assist him in achieving his dream. They struck upon a plan. They would ask to borrow money from the school master, as he was known to the students and in the community. This approach worked! When August said he was going with Gustav also, Mother Bertha was beside herself. She was sure she would never see her sons again. At the same time, she was highly supportive of the idea because it would mean that two of her sons would be migrating west to America instead of being drafted in the east for the czar's army.

With a small amount of money, fake passes, and a lot of courage, they left a tearful family in the dark of night. Traveling north to the Baltic Sea, they boarded a ship bound for England. The journey was not very eventful, except that hunger was their constant companion. Many times, August and Gustav thought of the many ways their mother had fixed potatoes to feed the children and stave off their complaints. They dreamed of the wonderful bread she baked so often in her open ovens.

Finally, with their arrival at Bristol, England, they needed to spend some time in quarantine and await passage to the United States. After they cleared the disease criteria, they were able travel freely as tourists across the region, and though they had no money, they could explore any area within walking distance. When the time came to leave for America, they boarded and headed across the Atlantic Ocean and up the St. Lawrence River on a ship named *The Airline*. They landed in Quebec and arrived in the United States at St. Albans, Vermont, during September of 1910. They finally made it to Wisconsin via the Great Lakes during that autumn.

Brother Emil and brother-in-law Julius had traveled to this area seeking their fortune. There was a town in northeastern Wisconsin named Underhill (or perhaps pronounced in German or Polish, Unterhill). Now they just needed to find the place where there were German-speaking people who could help them out and point them to jobs, because they needed to earn money to send back to their parents who had borrowed it to send their sons off to the United States. These were strong-headed boys!

They found Gillett and Underhill and were told there were jobs available in lumber camps to the north. If they knew how to work, they would be hired. Off they went for the winter, working together. They remained laboring at the lumber camp and toiling in the woods until the spring thaws sent them back to the Gillett area.

Often, a lonely Gustav found a stump where no one would bother him, where he could think about home and God. He remembered skating to school on the creek and how the school teacher was also training the children in their Christian studies. They memorized psalms, commandments, and songs. He remembered playing in the band for church services. The schoolhouse was also the church. Their traveling minister came only occasionally and questioned the pupils to check if they had studied well and were making good progress. Now that Gustav was here, and remembered these events with fondness.

He wrote letters to his family and sent some money to repay his debt. His connection to his family back in the old country was the train which brought supplies and mail. When Gustav and August left the camp in spring and went to Gillett, they needed to make some plans for the summer.

Only this time, when Gustav arrived at the lumber camp at Blackwell, he found that they needed someone to help cook, and Gustav accepted the challenge. He tied on the white half apron they presented to him and was given the position of assistant cookie, helping to prepare all the food and feed the lumberjacks. Here, he made friends with the camp manager and his wife who ran the kitchen and the rest of the camp shanty.

Brother August had fallen in love with a girl by the name of Olga Moser. She worked in a hotel in Upper Michigan, and August went there seeking work in the copper mines, as he needed to be near her.

In the lumber camp, there was plenty of opportunity for Gustav to speak German or Polish—and no place to spend your money, unless you played cards and gambled it away. When winter ended and the camp shut down, Gustav found himself at the Frederick farm again. The family was growing, and the children were Gustav's joy. In fact, the young children often chose him over their parents. Of course, the doling out of real discipline was not his role, so he had plenty of time for jokes that led to life lessons.

When the oldest Frederick boy found his friend's cigars, he secretly smoked them. Gustav waited and found the opportunity to cure him of smoking. He partly smoked a cigar and left it lying for a week, which seemed to add to the strength of the tobacco. When his small buddy found the cigar and tried it again, he became very sick. When Gustav confronted him the lad promised not to try it again.

When jobs opened in the Neenah paper mill, Gustav had picked up enough English to apply and was hired. He worked in the mill yard and also did work for the boss at his own home and yard. Then he had the chance to work at the Neenah foundry. He found that working inside under a roof wasn't what he wanted. He needed to work outside under the blue sky.

Still dissatisfied, he headed back to Gillett and his friends. About this time, August and Olga had married and settled in the Oconto Falls area. The brothers both worked for the Falls Paper Company for a time. Often, Gustav used the horse he had earned while working for the Fredericks to go over to Underhill and attend dances held in the hall. However, the call of the lumber camps continued for Gustav. Even later on, after he married and had a family, when the winter descended upon the land, Gustav often took his horses and went off to the lumber camps to do some lumberjacking. Working as a teamster, his job included skidding logs out of the woods and then loading them onto sleighs to get them to the railhead.

3

Gustav and Paulina

At the Underhill dances, Gustav noticed a very attractive, brown-haired, green-eyed shy girl, but he didn't get acquainted with her until the end of the year. He found himself dancing with her many times on a certain evening. It was her smile that won him over. She told him her name was Paulina Desterhoft. A week later, Gustav was back at Underhill hoping against hope that she would be there. Sure enough, there she was. He tried not to be too bold, lest she would turn away.

After the evening was over, he realized it was once again time to return to the lumber camp for the winter, and Gustav was sure he would never again see his dream girl. Winter dragged on—he did not even know where this Paulina lived. Well, in the spring he would get back to the Frederick's farm and he would find out!

Finally, spring came. With the snow melting and the ground thawing, the camp broke up for the year, and Gustav went back to Gillett. He returned to stay with the Frederick family. Somehow, he would talk to this family about the girl of his dreams. When he brought up the subject, he learned that Gottlieb Desterhoft had died and that the family was in need of a man around. He wondered where they lived and how he could tell Paulina his feelings. He had a fluttering sensation in his heart and hoped she felt the same about him.

One Sunday, he got dressed in his best clothes, got on his bicycle, and headed toward Pulcifer and the farm that the Frederick brothers told him about. The roads in those days were outsized dirt and gravel trails, so this was a several-hour trek. He had no idea how he would even begin a conversation. Of course, one thing was for sure, language would not be a barrier. He could use at least three variations of German and Polish if need be, for he had no idea what kind of person Paulina's mother, Ida Desterhoft, might be. While preparing for his visit and during his ride to her farm, he had questions in his mind. Would Ida be a hard or a soft woman? Would she hold conventional, old-country ideas and practices? How and in what ways would she be a tough protector of her daughter? Would he be welcomed into her house and perhaps into her family? Well, he would work to win her over with his charm, his smile, and his pleasant way. For on his ride over, he knew he wanted to have Paulina for his wife.

Breaking the ice was easier than he expected because the brothers were present and conversation was easy. In fact, he was invited to stay and share a meal. This was one of the customs in those days, as no one was sent away without food. He noticed, of course, that Paulina was in charge of the cooking, the chickens, carrying water, and doing so much of the work despite the fact she looked like she only weighed about 85 lbs. Her smile was very shy and beautiful. Gustav did not speak of marriage on that day because that would have been too bold.

Summer found him there many times. He eagerly showed his willingness to help with any of the work that needed to be done. During this time of working with Ida's family, there was also time to court Paulina. It may have been spending time with her while she did her many chores or perhaps sitting on the porch or the front steps, giving her an eye twinkle to find out a little more about this shy young woman. Gustav was totally taken with Paulina, and it was rumored that he flirted with her, whispering that he planned to ask her mother's consent for them to be wedded.

Finally, he was able to gather up his bravery and asked Ida for permission to marry her daughter. Ida said yes. So the date was set, and plans were made. The marriage would take place on September 26, 1914, at the Lutheran church in Gillett. Pastor Garrlock, who had confirmed Paulina, would marry the couple. Their attendants would be her friend Hulda Beyer, who would be the bridesmaid, and Paulina's cousin, also named Hulda. Paulina's brother Emil and Gustav's friend Adolph Jesse would be the groomsmen. So the plans were completed and in place. The wedding was small but very impressive. Paulina was dressed in lovely white splendor, lace attached, white veil with flowers and vines, and long white gloves. What a beautiful bride Gustav had found for himself—and her smile and personality won his heart for the many years to come.

TRAVELERS FROM THE OLD COUNTRY: MAKING IT IN AMERICA

For Gustav and Paulina, the young lovebirds, two could live almost as cheaply as one. Gustav worked hard with the Desterhoft family and cleared more land for cropping, building up the livestock herd to include hogs, cows, sheep, and horses. Of course, increasing the number of chickens and ducks resulted in more eggs and meat being available to the family. They tilled the garden area to make it a treasure plot of fruits and vegetables, planted fruit trees, and enlarged the fields. They also built outbuildings to house the animals and even added on to the house with a plan to build a second house across the field for Ida. Under Gustav's supervision, little time was wasted, as he had daily duties delegated for everyone. He listed every project and the work tasks to be done with timelines to bring their dreams to fruition. With Gustav's leadership, even Paulina's lazy brothers were forced to put in some time and effort on the farm.

Paulina took the lead in gardening and tending to the flocks of chickens and ducks. The household tasks such as washing, cleaning, and cooking were also a continued priority. With her mother, Paulina also mended and sewed clothes so that everyone had clean, wearable, and durable articles for working and going to church. There was much work to do. Water needed to be pumped and carried for household tasks and for the animals. Food needed canning and to be pickled or smoked to be preserved. Because there was no refrigeration, electricity, or central heat, sawing, splitting, and stacking wood was a necessary part of cooking and heating. The family was secure, as Gustav brought his creativity and a hard work ethic to get things done.

TRAVELERS FROM THE OLD COUNTRY: MAKING IT IN AMERICA

About this time, Paulina became pregnant with their first child. Martha was born in 1916, and her birth started their new family. Twin brothers, Henry and Herman, were born two years later. Henry's twin brother, Herman, died at eight months old of influenza. For some reason Herman's death was not easy for the family to process and put behind them. Death resulting from the flu was not uncommon, as no one went to the hospital, at least no one that the family knew. The doctor would only come to the house if he thought you could pay. Then in April of 1920, Hildegarde was born.

Initially, Paulina wouldn't allow the children to speak English. When Martha and Henry went to school, however, they first had to learn English before learning their lessons. Both Martha and Henry were held back a year because of this. Then Gustav put his foot down, and the rules changed. English became the language spoken at home.

By the early 1920s, the humble log cabin had been replaced with a two-story brick house to give shelter to the expanding family. The upstairs rooms, however, had no insulation or heat so in the wintertime they were as cold as can be. As the winter approached, added quilts were piled onto the beds to keep them warm. The upstairs was rarely used past Christmastime. During the winter, everyone slept downstairs—three to a bed with a double bed in the front room.

The front room, for the most part, was kept closed for Ida, or Grandma Desterhoft as she was known by the family members. She kept her furniture there, even though she had moved to an adjacent farm in the farmhouse that Emil had purchased for her. Why the front room was kept for her was always a puzzle. The downstairs rooms (in addition to the front room) for the family included a pantry, a kitchen, and two small bedrooms. It may have been part of the deal that Gustav struck with Ida when he took over the farm: continued support for Grandma, with a right to claim that front room to stay and sleep in if needed, along with an agreed-upon salary for her living expenses.

The year 1925, must have been very hard for my mother, because she was pregnant with the family with three kids: Martha was ten, Henry was eight, and Hildegarde was six. The ongoing work load and raising three children and then my birth made it a difficult burden for her to bear. For the family however, life was made easier by the mid-1920's as the farm was producing, food was plentiful, and the expectations were small. This was no wonder, as my earliest memories were that we didn't own a radio or telephone, and of course television hadn't even been invented at that time

It was up to us to use our creative energies for the dreams we wanted for ourselves going forward. Our reading came from something called the "Feibal." This was a German-English book that would help with pronunciations. The library at school supplied lots of good things, even copies of the beloved *National Geographic*.

Without any resources for medicine, the family extensively used home remedies to deal with injuries and address illness. For a toothache, a whole clove was kept on the infected tooth area. For bad cuts, a sack with cow manure would be wrapped around the injured area to draw out any infection. Usually this was an overnight application. Camphor was another remedy for stomach ills and colds.

Pieces of camphor bark were dissolved in water and then the concoction was swallowed to deal with stomachaches. Camphor was also wrapped in a cloth and used as a scarf and pinned around the neck helped to take care of sore throats. If this didn't work, a boiled honey and onion mix might be eaten to assist the cold to leave your body. Finally, if these remedies failed to cure the cold, skunk oil or Vicks Vapor Rub was smeared across the neck, chest, and back.

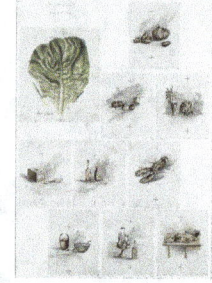

4

Herman's Story

One of the area families we visited from time to time was a husband and his wife, Herman and Ida. They lived approximately six miles from our farm. Herman and his brother arrived in the United States and Wisconsin about the same year as Gust and August did. Herman's story was likely one that happened to others at that time. Herman had a wife and child that he had left in Europe with the promise to send for them as soon as he had work and a place to live. Herman found that work in the woods and was faithfully paid by the lumber camp owners. But if you didn't hide and carefully guard your money, well, guess what happened? Everyone was so poor, and his paid wages were stolen by someone in that camp. The result was that there was not enough money in his wallet to send for his spouse and child who were still living in Europe.

Year after year passed, and he had no communication with his wife, as Herman couldn't read or write. He depended upon others to help him with this, but could he trust them? As the past began to fade, he met Ida, and some of his loneliness left him. They married and she was a fine woman and a good partner. They were blessed with two children. They spent about fifteen years together, and then Ida passed away. Herman was once again empty and lonely.

Several years later, he met Elise. Now, she was very different. Although she was raised in the country, she dressed and lived the part of a city girl. But she made Herman happy. After just a couple of years of caring for each other, tragedy struck: Elise's only sister and remaining family member died. This caused Elise to go into severe depression. Within a year she suffered a heart problem and suddenly passed away. Only later was the pill bottle and note found, which made it evident that she had ended her own life. Could this have been true? There was so much to live for, but her pain and depression seemed stronger than continuing on in life.

For Herman, the loneliness of life without a partner was great. What could he do but to begin searching once again? By this time, Herman was no longer a young man. His children were on their own; they were grown and had moved to live in the city. As fate would have it, a sweet unmarried lady by the name of Della lived in the neighborhood. She was willing to become Herman's wife and new partner. After about five years with Della, Herman passed away. This left a big emptiness in my parents' life. This was just one of the stories of those German-speaking immigrants who were beginning to die of age-related illnesses.

The tragedy of Herman's story was that he came to America with the intent to bring his family here as he was settled in and financially stable. Unfortunately, the separation from his family moved from a temporary state and became permanent. For everyone, the key to the good life lays with the heartfelt need to stay aware of priorities and responsibilities while remaining true to those principles. For Herman, life and life circumstances claimed his principles and he was reduced to live life for the present without thinking of the past and planning for the future. There is a lesson here for all of us.

5

Farming Times

My parents, Gustav and Pauline, lived on a farm—the hilliest in the Pulcifer area; or so we thought. Well it really wasn't Pulcifer, as it wasn't in Shawano County, but rather in Oconto County, and our mailing address was Gillett, Wisconsin. However, our beloved school was at Pulcifer, and most of our best friends and buddies were from that area.

Most of Gustav and Paulina's friends were German speaking. Of course, in our area there were at least three dialects: high German, low German, and central German. These dialects were based on the region of Germany that these neighbors originated from.

Paulina's oldest brother, Ferdinand, disappeared from the family shortly after the death of her father. Where he went or what sort of life he had we don't know. We never heard from him. He didn't write, never contacted the family, and never came around to visit my grandma.

Everyone we knew was as poor as we were. My father and mother owned about eighty acres, or was it the money lender who owned us?

They planted fields of green beans (as a young girl, the fields seemed huge), which were picked by hand. We earned money by the backbreaking toil of picking beans nearly every day, all summer long. Dad and Mother paid us one and one-half cents a pound for picking, and we kept track of the sacks we put our beans in. These were feed sacks or the kind used to carry oats. Sometimes, it would seem the older ones in the family cheated, as their sacks always filled before mine.

Those were long, hot days, and that is when the beans grew best. We were all as brown as our shoes, and in those days, it was not very fashionable to get a tan. But the payoff came in mid-December when the bean payments arrived. We sat for hours with the Sears & Roebuck Chicago mail order catalog, and sometimes we could borrow Spiegel's. These catalogs were standard in most homes.

We earned enough to buy clothes. These were the true dream books, and even though we had only six or eight dollars, there were so many possibilities. I could get shoes and one dress or perhaps a new coat if there was no hand-me-down just then. Maybe it would be two new dresses this year.

We knew about oranges, grapefruit, and bananas, but seldom had any. However, when they gave out the Christmas bags at the church program, it contained a great variety of treats. This included a few mixed nuts, some hard candy, a few angel-food candies, perhaps an apple, and always an orange. What a gift that Christmas bag was! We kept it and tried to make it last for weeks. Sometimes, I was sure Ruth got into mine and took some of my best stuff. I would then attack her while Mother hurriedly came to the rescue. She would separate us in an instant and restore the peace.

Even where we lived influenced us so much. Our long side road made it necessary to be good neighbors with the Miller family who lived across from our farm, but they were far enough away so we really couldn't see all that happened at their place. We would see the lantern go up to the house at the end of milking time— or the flashlight coming toward our drive. Our family didn't own any flashlights. The Millers seemed to have more money, in spite of the death of their dad, as all of the twelve children were several years older than me. This was not to say that they were well off. With so many children, they would report that they ate potatoes at every meal. While they had a super large kitchen table, there were a limited number of chairs. As the youngest, Walter had to stand at his table place to eat. When his oldest brother left home, only then did he get a chair to sit at the table.

Even though Alvin and Walter were older than me, we were good friends. They were also so very helpful. They helped pitch hay or put up shocks of grain. We went sleigh riding in the winter and would swim together almost every night in the summer. We also walked to school together.

When we got to school, the scene would change. They went off with their friends, and I spent time with mine. At noon or lunchtime, which lasted one hour, Alvin and Walter had small jobs in town shoveling snow and whatever else, and they always seemed to have a little money for candy. Two cents bought a lot of sweets. Oftentimes, Walter would come past my desk at school to share some candy with me.

During the summer of 1930, there was a bad storm one afternoon, and lightning struck the barn. It was immediately engulfed in flames. My brother Henry discovered this catastrophe and immediately ran to the neighbors to get help. They had a car and he raced over to the adjacent farm where my dad, Gustav, was plowing a field. He dropped everything and came back home in a great hurry. Unfortunately, the barn couldn't be saved. All the calves, pigs, chickens, and the stored feed perished in the fire. The cows were out in the pasture, so they were safe. The barn had to be rebuilt and was constructed before the onset of winter. But with no chickens, the family missed out on eggs and fried chicken until the flock could be reestablished.

Shortly before I went to school, my sister Ruth was born. Or perhaps her birth happened when I was in first grade. She was precious and a pain. This was the same situation I found with my older sisters. But when she grew older, Ruth and I did lots of playing together; making snow houses, cutting paper dolls, and trading ideas for ways to pass the time.

In the summer, we had another awful job of watching cows. I hate even thinking about it today because it still makes me very nervous and angry. It meant taking the herd of cows to a pasture, a field without fences, with the charge to keep them from straying off and getting into the adjacent cropland ... by standing there for entirely too long. This could last a whole hour or extend into what seemed like an eternity. Sometimes we were allowed to take a clock, and then we could skimp on the length of the boring time. If instead, we had to wait to hear a yell from the farmyard; well, that took what seemed like forever because we were sure they forgot to call us to bring the cows home. There were no shade trees, and this job had to be done every day. We had an umbrella, but that was extra baggage because we needed a jacket to sit on, a long stick to keep the cattle in check and, sometimes, and our old alarm clock for keeping time.

After the cows were chased out to the pasture, Ruth and I spent time near the rock pile located in the area, pretending we had special stones with embedded diamonds and a huge desk. We could be bankers, teachers, or very rich people. There was also the creek where we could gaze until we saw the fish or watched the assorted reflections in the watery mirror.

Then it was time to hurry home to hoe the weeds in the garden. That garden had everything, which included a large strawberry patch. Soft drinks and soda were unheard of in our house, but we had strawberry juice to drink in season. Mmmm, fresh strawberries! The taste beat any soft drinks. We had an orchard with cherry, plum, and apple trees. These trees had pitch running on the limbs, and we chewed that and ate it. It was the best gum!

Despite the work, summers were often carefree. We were barefoot and brown from the sun and really laid back—even with the Millers' bees were always buzzing around. They had lots of hives, and when we went to swim, we had to go through their cow yard where the hives were kept. More than once we would get stung by those bees. The river called, and even the grown-ups went down to the river because it was fun and it was also our summer bathtub. Very few people in our area had the luxury of an indoor bathtub. In the late evenings, we sat on the porch and then as the dark descended, we would fall into our beds. At that time, we had no electricity. This meant no lights in the house, the barn, or the yard. It also required some ingenuity since there was no refrigeration or pumping motors for moving water to where it was needed. This was done entirely by hand, along with carrying pails and pots for watering animals, cooking, and washing.

At the end of the summer, it was time for threshing the grain for the harvest. It brought on real excitement. Mother was really busy because the workmen stayed right at the farm—as many as ten or twelve extra men to cook for, usually three full meals and sometimes an extra lunch.

How did Mother do it without a refrigerator? Everything started from scratch on that day. Chickens were butchered, cleaned, and roasted, and bread and cakes were baked as well. There were dishes

TRAVELERS FROM THE OLD COUNTRY: MAKING IT IN AMERICA

to be washed, and water and wood needed to be carried. Everyone who was able to got really busy. Sometimes one of the kids had to shovel the grain. The threshing machine was a huge thing with a steam engine for power. There was a team of horses dedicated to pulling a water wagon, as the steam engine seemed to continually need refilling. They got water from the river or a tank, and we had to pump it entirely by hand. It was also very dirty with dust and chaff everywhere, especially in the water pails, as the pump was near the barn. The men would come into the house with dirt in their pant cuffs and their faces black with soot or grain dust. Then the harvesting day or days were over and we had completed the big grain reaping job.

Summer also held one other real big event. That was the Fourth of July holiday! Dad would always manage to procure some firecrackers, and he taught us to stand on the porch, light the firecrackers with a large farmer match, and throw it hard while covering our ears. At night we left for town and the park. The kids rode in the back of the truck. What a thrill it was to hear the merry-go-round music, and the sights and sounds of the carnival. We could earn some money pulling weeds from the oats fields, so we'd arrive at the carnival with at least a quarter to hold and wonder how to spend it. For five cents, we could get two merry-go-round tickets, and five cents would also buy a double-dip ice cream cone. If we were careful, we would even have a little money to bring home.

It was nice to have a Grandma to visit. Her house was not too far away, and we would often walk through the fields and cross some steep hills to reach the farm. Grandma would always use one of us kids to help bake a cake. In fact, she taught me really well. She would have me get the bowl, two eggs, and the pitcher of milk that she always stored in the cellar. After adding the flour to the bowl, she would pour a splash of this and add a dash of that, and I would beat the mix together. "Oh, but wait," she'd say. "We need to add some wood to the stove." It had no dials, so it was not easy to know how much wood to put in that cook stove. She would stick her hand into the oven to check the temperature, and then when the heat level was correct, we would put the cake in. It always turned out just right.

Grandma Desterhoft was a short but forceful lady. She had had a tough life. She came to the United States from Warsaw in 1903 late in pregnancy with nothing more than a steamer trunk, a husband, and two small kids. It must have been some experience. Fifteen years later, her husband died and she must have wondered where to turn. She never remarried—spending the balance of her life keeping house and bossing her grown sons who actually didn't listen anyway. But she taught her granddaughters how to bake cakes and apple pies!

TRAVELERS FROM THE OLD COUNTRY: MAKING IT IN AMERICA

When I was about thirteen, Grandma Desterhoft became bedridden with what was perhaps a light stroke. My sister Hildegarde was her nurse. I felt like Hildegarde had a very heavy job on her hands. After about a year and one half of illness, Grandma died at home. In those days, when people died, they brought the body home in the casket and placed it in the middle of the living room. I stayed with Hildegarde that night, and it was a very scary night for me. Grandma's dead body was downstairs, and our bed was upstairs right over the casket. That was before I realized that living people are far more dangerous than the dead.

I remember Grandma for other things also. This was the only grandma I ever knew. She never held me on her lap or hugged or kissed me. She never told me she loved me. I wondered if it was because I was too much trouble or looked so plain. She did say I was far too skinny. I also overheard Grandma complain to my mom about all the kids we had in our family. We were the only grandchildren she ever had, and I thought she should just enjoy us, but she had no time to spoil kids. Or was this only my imagination? We could always find peppermint candy on her table, and at Christmastime, our only rag doll had a new body and new clothes, made by Grandma.

One Christmas, my uncle Emil made a doll crib, and there was a quilt in that bed. Uncle Emil would stop by after hauling milk and tease Ruth and me. He would tell jokes, have a good laugh with us, and perhaps flash some money our way, at times giving us nickels or dimes. For Emil, his life started out with so much possibility and ended with so much misfortune.

Emil, Gust, and Albert lived on the beautiful farm Emil

purchased. He bought it with the help of my dad, Gustav. After some years of working together with Grandma—cooking, washing, and cleaning along with working the farm—they fell under the spell of alcohol. In spite of Grandma's scolding, as if that did any good, alcohol entered the lives of the young men, and it wasn't a good influence on the body, the brain, or their family relationships.

Things and times changed as Gust left and went to work in the big city of Milwaukee, a long way from Gillett; it seemed that it was located just this side of the moon. There, he found and married a wife. That left Albert, Emil, and the hired help to work the farm. Things worked out fine until Emil married his girlfriend, Evelyn, and this was a terrible mismatch. She did not know how to keep a house clean, or for that matter how to keep her own body clean. When their first child, Darlene, was born, Evelyn did not keep the baby clean either. Emil would come over to our house with his dirty baby girl, dressed in dirty clothes, and riding in a foul-smelling baby buggy. This was so upsetting to my mother, and she scolded Emil. She said, "First clean and feed the baby. Then wash every last thing. Get that buggy cleaned up, and set it in the sun to dry with a fresh breeze to air it out."

Emil and Evelyn had a second baby, and they named him Lawrence. Next, Emil sold the farm and bought a bar in town. What a mistake that turned out to be. The hours were irregular; and Emil imbibed much of the product. He couldn't create a set of regular customers because he didn't work to set up a lively social atmosphere where people would come for both the beer and the conversation. He was soon indebted to the distributors and lenders while at the same time experiencing decreasing revenues.

Next, twin girls were born. They were named Shirley and Janet.

(It makes me nervous just thinking about this). Conditions in their home and business did not improve. Drinks were so available and became the center of Emil and Evelyn's life. Soon Emil sold the bar and bought another one forty-five miles to the west.

In the meantime, the care of the babies was neglected. The baby bottle would turn sour as the milk fermented, and it was never cleaned in a thorough way. One of the twins, Shirley, died. In our family, it was said that the cause of death was due to malnutrition. How my mom suffered to watch this entire scene taking place. By this time, I was married and had two children. I couldn't believe or understand such neglect.

Things for Emil did not improve. Just beyond the bar was a small river with lots of stones at the edges along the riverbank. The children would go there to play. The youngest girl, Janet, was about five years old. As there was no adult supervision, she slipped and fell into the river and drowned.

Life for Emil then moved from bad to worse. Emil loved to tease, and this was often a source of trouble for him. There was a man who hung around in the bar and confessed all his troubles to Emil. His girlfriend was pregnant and what could he do? Emil laughed, teased, and joked with him about the situation, probably thinking that to take this approach would help lighten the load. The man left the bar and became angrier by the moment. When he reached his home he agonized about his troubles, and his resentment over his situation and Emil's response built to a boiling point. He grabbed his gun and went back to the bar with a plan. He proceeded to use the gun to shoot and kill Emil at the bar. He confessed to the police, and when the hearing and trial was held, he was found guilty and sentenced to a substantial prison term.

This experience stayed with my mom for the rest of her life. All she could say was what a waste of life that had been. Across our family, the death of Emil also affected us. We said, "Let's go forward; the past is over." Even though saying this did not alleviate the pain of this tragedy.

Some years later, friends told me that Evelyn cooked in a bar and restaurant somewhere in western Wisconsin. I never believed that; I thought it was a joke. How could she even work in a restaurant if she never cared about or demonstrated that she knew about being clean? I really don't know.

In spite of this heartbreak, life moved on. However, we really lost that part of my mom's family. I often wonder where they went and how this could have happened to my mother's brothers. What went wrong? My mother's siblings made choices that weren't keeping with the family traditions. In the end, one of Mom's brothers disappeared, one was shot, and two moved to the big city. They didn't continue their lives on the farm, remain in the area, or stay connected to the family.

It was very hard to be a successful farmer in those days. Everyone had horse-drawn machines, and for the most part, the farmer walked for hours behind plows, drags, and other field equipment. Cows were milked by hand, and most people owned ten or twelve cattle. We also had sheep, pigs, and chickens. The chickens were a great help because the eggs provided a real cash crop. Besides having fresh chicken for meals and eggs for our own use, those eggs were sold for groceries. About the only things we bought were yeast, salt, sugar, and a little coffee and tea. Additionally, on the store list was kerosene for the lamps and lanterns.

Winters were so difficult. The old car (truck) was placed on blocks of wood (to keep the tires from sinking into the ground) from right after Christmas until spring. Anywhere we went, it meant we walked or rode with the horses.

I remember going in the sleigh to Grandma's house or to Uncle August and Aunt Olga's. We had heavy blankets wrapped around us. Most of the winter was spent right at home. Even church was not attended after Christmas until spring and Easter came. Occasionally, though, we walked to Sunday school in the wintertime.

Ruth and I spent many evenings building houses from blocks of snow. They usually lasted about two days before they caved in, or we were distracted by some other sport or pastime. Sometimes our brother would hitch the dog to our sled. The dog resisted the harness and would turn around and try to bite us or go crazy, dragging us every which way. Once, Henry tried making skis. They weighed a ton and the ends turned up a bit. Four or five of us would have to take turns trying them out.

One winter I remember well. When a major snowstorm came, we would often wait for days to have the road plowed. This one time, all the children (except Ruth who was too young) from the neighborhood went sledding on the main highway just after a huge snowstorm. This stretch of the highway featured an incredible hill and was a natural place to ride downhill at great speeds. One person stood guard to watch for cars while the others piled on sleds and flew down the road. Highways were never salted in those days. Usually there was a buildup of snow, and it was packed hard by the few cars that drove there in winter. Finally, we could see lights coming over the hill and the loud roar of an engine. Wow, it wasn't a car or a truck; it was the county's snowplow with the side wing blade. The side wing would throw the snow off the road and make a continuous ridge about four feet high at the ditch or on the side of the highway. All the kids who were walking to school fought for the right to walk up on the crest. Sometimes you could nearly touch the telephone wires if the snow stacked up after several snowstorms hit the area.

My brother Melvin had been born the year I started high school. He was a very sweet baby, and we all enjoyed him beyond telling. One of my class projects involved childcare, and I really did a lot of helping my mom assist in washing, feeding, and changing my baby brother. The class provided many valuable skills and ideas in the caring and development of infants.

TRAVELERS FROM THE OLD COUNTRY: MAKING IT IN AMERICA

Diapers and clothes were washed by hand. It was at this time that we needed to move from the old home farm. I had to quit high school for a year and never had the chance to go back to finish. I was so sad. But all the changes that were taking place made me realize I needed to help at home. Oh, I rebelled plenty at first. My salvation was a Madison organization where I would write to request library books. I would travel or do whatever was needed to get possession of those precious books. This service was free, and I only needed return postage. Every two weeks brought me a new supply.

When we moved to the new farm, there were neighbors to meet and new relationships, friendships, and acquaintances to be made. This farm had electricity and a telephone. An important addition was a pump house, which was where we would wash our clothes. Mother had a washing machine we could convert to run with our new toy, electricity. By this time Martha, Henry, and Hildegard were married. Along with the joy, horror of all horrors, Henry was in a battle of divorce. In those years, few people were doing this—at least no one in our family.

It was 1943, and while going to church in Gillett, I saw a very handsome guy sitting with his mother, dad, a young lady, and another fellow about twenty-five or twenty-six years old. I figured this handsome guy was married to the lady, so I tried to dismiss him from my mind. About a week later, Martha came by to untangle the web and tell me that Handsome was really Adolph Schultz, an eligible bachelor. These were WWII years, and most of the young fellows were off to serve their country, but Adolph had just returned from California where he had been working at the Lockheed aircraft plant. The person that I thought he was married to was actually his sister, Tillie. She was married to that other fellow (my future brother-in-law, Gust) who had been sitting with them in the church pew. Tillie was a good friend of my sister Martha. Little did I realize then that this was the beginning of my own romance journey.

6

Stories from my Family with Adolph

After that first glance at that handsome man came several friendly conversations and pleasant encounters. This led to a couple of dates to movies and dancing and then getting those feelings of love embedded in my heart and soul. An early memory of the courting times was at the movie house, where I had come with my sister as my date and saw Adolph there with his date. We saw each other there and after a bit of flirting, disobeyed the rule that you always go home with whom you came. This may have been a sign that love overcomes any ordinary rules; we abandoned our dates and left the movie with each other.

The dating became more frequent and an inevitability of deeper love moved us to our marriage. After we married, it seemed that our destiny was to be farmers. The early years of our marriage were rather lean and provided a struggle with prioritizing the bills; the most necessary had to be paid first. This was combined with much hard work as we found and purchased a property of two hundred acres but with no buildings. This meant building the house, the garage, the barn and all the outbuildings even as we acquired cattle and the farm equipment and made sure we were working the land to plant and harvest the crops.

Our story then extended to include our children, Duane and Dean, making us a family with all the joys and tribulations associated with trying to make a living. Many people would mix up their names; which one was Duane and which was Dean? Their own mother and dad could also get caught up in this, although we always did know one from the other. With farm life, we had the typical struggles of many young families. We had to make sure we had feed for the cattle. And at the same time, we had to balance this with the new shoes needed for the children. Or would it be a baseball glove which the boys had saved up to buy? Of course, we managed to be very happy in spite of not having lots of new stuff.

We always had a farm dog and barn cats. The children loved their pets, but especially loved the dog as their pal. When I heard the dog barking and barking, I knew the children had climbed up on something that the dog could not access and they were teasing him by making strange sounds or silly faces. When they tired of that game or thought the dog had been barking for long enough, they would stop and the dog seemed to understand.

The boys also built an awful looking shack next to the road. It was somehow nailed together between some trees that stood on the shoulder of the ditch. They used a mix of boards, paneling, and tar paper to construct it. The place was used as a hideout, a palace, an office, and whatever else happened to appear in their minds as they played. After a couple of months, they grew tired of it. It was a very happy day for me when, with the help of their father, the shack was torn down and totally deconstructed.

They seemed to always find things to do and were happy with the adventuring around the yard and the farm. An early example of this was when preschooler Duane used a hammer and some nails to pound together some old boards. He took this supposed sculpture and pounded it into the ground in the front yard. We did not have much traffic on that town road but imagine our chagrin when a guy stopped in and, looking at the makeshift item, asked if that was the sign stating that our farm was for sale. We said no to the idea that we were selling the place, and as he left, we made Duane take that thingamajig down to the back of the garage.

The beginning of their education started at Sunny Slope School. Their favorite teacher was Mrs. Nelson and her balanced and reasonable approach to teaching and learning gave them a good start. For a one room country school with limited resources, her creativity and the excitement that she brought to the classroom was infectious to all the students. She knew when to get strict and when to remain flexible, always keeping the education and the development of her students front and center. The school closed when Duane was finishing the fifth grade but both boys were fortunate to have Mrs. Nelson for their teacher during their entire time at the school.

Our favorite family date on a Friday night was to visit the community library and after doing some browsing, each family member would choose two or three books. We then would come home to have some quiet reading time. It was a golden time for everyone to start one of the books borrowed and checked out that evening. One of my dreams was that our children would go to college. Adolph and I sincerely agreed on that point without any doubts.

One time, Dean came home to ask how old one must be in order to quit school. I quickly told him to forget that thought because that was not going to happen. Duane came home from school another time to tell me how unfair it was he needed to read more books than one of his other classmates. I asked if he was capable and he replied, "But it's not fair." My response was, "Aren't you ever a fortunate student."

How empty the house seemed when the children left for college. However, we have never tired of our respect for, and awe of, education. For me to get to attend the college graduations of our children and then our grandchildren was a thrill and a treasure of my lifetime. I think of my grandmother and mother who had such limited ability to read and write, to my own dreams of high school graduation being dashed by life's realities. Those graduation celebrations were my version of getting to the mountain top. To see all my children and grandchildren with their college degrees and professional successes in their lives has made life so worthwhile and fulfilling.

7

Reflections: An Open Letter to My Family

In 2012, about the time I finished the first round of my cancer treatments, I found the rehabilitation experience gave me some time to think and wonder about life and death. I did think that I was dying. For all the thought searching I have done, I cannot specifically call up the memory of writing this letter. But in organizing some of my papers, I came across this letter and realized that it could apply to the present as well as when I wrote it.

The memory of the life story of Adolph and Emma (Reichwald) Schultz belongs to those who lived it. As parents and grandparents, we loved our family with all our hearts. We made plenty of mistakes and hope we will be forgiven for every one of them.

Your dad/grandpa as a person was full of humble pride in all the accomplishments that his family made. And this also goes for me.

We could hardly wait for the news to see who from our family was in the spotlight just then or perhaps next in line for a celebration of an accomplishment or a success. We both were awed by education, and I wished that Grandpa Adolph could have lived to see the picture of our family as it played out and to dr

The years after Adolph's death reshaped my life. I needed so much help from my family. They willingly came forward, and I thank each and every one of you for that. I realize my body will soon stop existing, but what will happen to my inner self and where did that part of me come from?

What a wonder our bodies are and how we can learn to adapt. I just recently heard of a farmer who passed away. He had no arms yet invented ways to do his chores and daily tasks. I also know of an organization of painters; they are known as *Mouth and Foot Painting Artists*. What courage and strength it must take to say, "I can and I will." My question is, am I personally grateful?

I recently read in a biology book about all the capabilities of our brain. It can tell our hands to do their duties with just a simple command; a thought. With this we can move our hands, our legs, and our bodies. At the same time, we can ensure that all the bodily functions take place, some that we may not even be aware of. All except for our thoughts, which need our active thinking to achieve. (Of course this is not the latest in the advances being made so we will need to wait as science comes through with new conclusions.) As an example, I'm thinking of the dimension of me that is capable of writing thoughts, how is it organized and that it all works together in harmony. Thoughts are an inseparable aspect of the brain that sends messages to my hand to record the ideas with words on the page. Well, you get the picture.

Recently I reread the book *This I believe*. This, in turn, prompted me to write this short letter. Everyone should put together his or her thoughts of what we believe. I believe I was born for a purpose. I'm not sure what that purpose was. Perhaps my function was to be a daughter, a sister, a wife, a mother, a grandmother, a great-grandmother, a friend, a neighbor, etc. Each of these roles taught me lessons, and these are not written down in any books. Maybe that was my purpose—being the best that I know how to be, and of course falling far short.

As I write this, I know that soon my inner self will leave this body. It will go somewhere back to my Creator. I know I am not worthy to stand in His presence. I need an Advocate, and I have one in Jesus. I wish each one of you, as you examine yourself, will also wonder and choose wisely. For now, the lesson is, be a good neighbor. Help care for the less fortunate. Love each other. Forgive each other's faults. This will make life sweet. I leave you with the hope that you will, each one of you. And realize that I had many favorites in our family; each one of you is my favorite.

May my God richly bless each of you,
Grandma Emma

END

About this Book and Author

About this Book

Anyone who is interested in their family roots will want to join Emma as she traces her family's trek to America. The *Travelers from the Old Country: Making it in America* paints the picture of her mother and father in the early twentieth century as new arrivals establishing a homestead and settling into a new life. The story takes us back to the times before electricity and modern conveniences, providing the reader with insights into the life and times of Emma and her family. Joyful vignettes of these throwback, simpler days are intertwined with moments of inevitable human suffering, the trials and tribulations that were an ever-present part of their lives. The story relates the never-ending optimism and faith brought by these immigrants at the turn of the century and that which they passed on to their children and grandchildren. It is a shared story of endurance and persistence that is common with so many brave souls who willingly cut ties with their extended families and relationships to adventure to America and begin a new life. It is indeed a story common to many people even in the present. The need to escape war and abuse provides the reader with a close-up and genuine understanding of why every immigrant will take a risky path to an unknown future to get to a place that may offer a bit of peace and hope.

About the Author

Emma Reichwald Schultz has been a lifelong resident of northeastern Wisconsin. She married Adolph Schultz back in the day and raised two sons on a farm near Oconto Falls. She has always been active in her church and area civic affairs. She also was a volunteer for many years in the Oconto County Home Respite Care organization. She still lives in the Oconto Falls area. This is her first book originally written for her family to set down a printed record of her memories.

www.ingramcontent.com/pod-product-compliance
Lightning Source LLC
Chambersburg PA
CBHW070744060526
44119CB00091B/411/J